Table of Contents

4

Tornadoes

by Matt Doeden

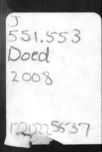

Lerner Publications Company • Minneapolis

Photo Acknowledgments

The images in this book are used with the permission of: © Photodisc/Getty Images, pp. 1, 9, all backgrounds; © Gene & Karen Rhoden/Visuals Unlimited, pp. 4, 6, 13, 27; © Mark Newman/SuperStock, p. 8; © Jim Reed/ Science Faction/Getty Images, p. 10; © Carsten Peter/National Geographic/Getty Images, p. 11; AP Photo/ Wayne Hanna, p. 12; © Chuck Doswell/Visuals Unlimited, pp. 14, 17; AP Photo/The Reporter, Don Lloyd, p. 16; © SuperStock, Inc./SuperStock, p. 18; AP Photo/Danny Johnston, p. 20; © Sam Lund/Independent Picture Service, p. 21; © Digitalprofile/ZUMA Press, p. 22; AP Photo/Messenger-Inquirer, Jenny Sevcik, p. 23; © Winfried Heinze/Red Cover/Getty Images, p. 24; AP Photo/The Advocate Messenger, Clay Jackson, p. 25; © John-Francis Bourke/zefa/CORBIS, p. 26.

Front Cover: © Paul & Lindamarie Ambrose/Taxi/Getty Images.
Back Cover: © Photodisc/Getty Images.

Text copyright © 2008 by Lerner Publishing Group, Inc.

Lerner Publications Company
A division of Lerner Publishing Group, Inc.
241 First Avenue North
Minneapolis, MN 55401

Website address: www.lernerbooks.com

Words in **bold type** are explained in a glossary on page 31.

Library of Congress Cataloging-in-Publication Data

Doeden, Matt.
    Tornadoes / by Matt Doeden.
       p.   cm. — (Pull ahead books—forces of nature)
    Includes index.
    ISBN 978–0–8225–7910–6 (lib. bdg. : alk. paper)
    1. Tornadoes—Juvenile literature. I. Title.
QC955.2.D64 2008
551.55'3—dc22   2007024905

Manufactured in the United States of America
1 2 3 4 5 6 – JR – 13 12 11 10 09 08

What Is a Tornado?

Storm sirens wail. The wind howls. What is happening? A **tornado** has been spotted! A tornado is a dangerous, spinning windstorm. Tornadoes are also called twisters. How do tornadoes form?

A supercell thunderstorm

How Tornadoes Start

Most tornadoes form inside powerful **thunderstorms**. These strong storms are called **supercells**. They form when **masses** of warm, wet air meet masses of cool, dry air. The warm and cold air masses travel at different speeds. They travel in different directions. A difference in wind speed or direction is called **wind shear**.

Warm air is lighter than cool air.
Warm air rises above cool air.

Rising warm air helps birds such as eagles fly high into the sky.

Rising warm air is called an **updraft**. As the warm air rises, it cools. The water in the air forms huge clouds.

Wind shear makes warm and cool air masses turn. They **rotate** around each other.

Sometimes an updraft hits the rotating air. The updraft makes the rotating air stand up like a spinning top.

This rotating air dips down below the
storm clouds. It touches the ground.

It has become a tornado.

A tornado in Texas

Where and When Tornadoes Happen

Tornadoes can form almost anywhere. But they are most common in the midwestern and southern parts of the United States. Many tornadoes strike an area called Tornado Alley. It includes Texas, Oklahoma, Kansas, and other states.

Tornadoes can happen almost any time of year. But most of them form during the spring and summer months.

During these seasons, the weather is often very warm. Warm weather makes storms stronger.

Buildings destroyed by a tornado

Staying Safe

Tornadoes can cause a lot of **damage**. They can tear apart houses. They can pick up cars. They can destroy whole towns. How do people stay safe during a tornado?

Most towns and cities have warning sirens. Scientists track storms. If they think a tornado may form, they tell people to turn on the sirens.

This scientist is looking for places where tornadoes may form.

Warning sirens make a loud noise.
When people hear a siren, they go to a
safe place.

People inside buildings should stay away from windows. A tornado can break windows. Sharp bits of broken glass may fly through the air.

A tornado's winds broke these windows.

This family is staying in the basement during a storm.

The safest place in a house is the basement. If a house doesn't have a basement, the lowest floor is safest.

Rooms in the middle of a house may be safe. They are safer than rooms along the outside walls.

A small bathroom with no windows can be a safe place to go during a storm.

These kids are practicing what to do if a tornado forms when they are at school.

In schools and other large buildings, people are safest in hallways.

People who are driving should stop their cars. They should go inside a strong building. If no building is near, they should lie flat on the ground.

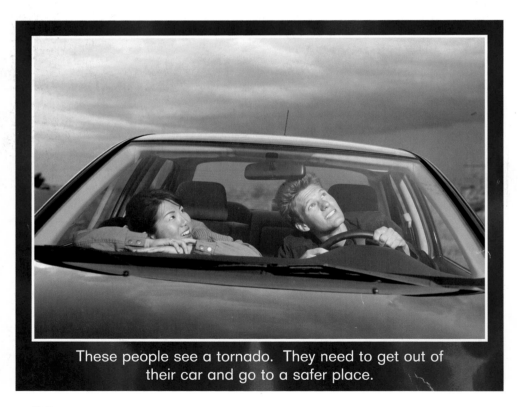

These people see a tornado. They need to get out of their car and go to a safer place.

Tornadoes are powerful. They are nature's most dangerous storms. But people can stay safe if they know what to do when a tornado forms.

MORE ABOUT TORNADOES

Scientists use the Enhanced Fujita scale to measure tornadoes. A weak tornado is ranked EF0. The speed of its winds is less than 85 miles per hour. The tornado's rating climbs as it grows stronger. The strongest tornadoes are ranked EF5. Their winds rotate faster than 200 miles per hour.

EF Number	Wind Speed (miles per hour)	Amount of Damage
0	65 to 85	Branches are broken off trees. Some chimneys are damaged.
1	86 to 110	Mobile homes are turned upside down. Cars are pushed off roads.
2	111 to 135	Roofs are torn off some houses. Mobile homes are destroyed. Large trees are blown down.
3	136 to 165	Roofs and some walls are torn off strong houses. Trains are knocked over. Most trees are blown down.
4	166 to 200	Strong houses are flattened. Weaker houses are thrown through the air.
5	more than 200	Strong houses are thrown through the air. Cars are thrown long distances.

Tornado Facts

- Most tornadoes last only 5 to 10 minutes. Very strong tornadoes may last for hours and travel more than 100 miles.

- About 1,000 tornadoes are reported every year in the United States.

- Some tornadoes form above water. These tornadoes are called waterspouts.

- Most tornadoes happen between 3:00 P.M. and 7:00 P.M. This is usually the warmest part of the day.

- A tornado watch means conditions are right for a tornado to form. A tornado warning means a tornado has been spotted or one seems to be forming in a storm.

Further Reading

Books

Jango-Cohen, Judith. *Why Does It Rain?* Minneapolis: Millbrook Press, 2006.

Miles, Elizabeth. *Forecasting the Weather*. Chicago: Heinemann, 2006.

Orme, David, and Helen Orme. *Tornadoes*. New York: Children's Press, 2005.

Simon, Seymour. *Tornadoes*. New York: HarperTrophy, 2001.

Websites

Tornadoes
http://www.fema.gov/kids/tornado.htm
This website has important information about tornadoes and what to do if a tornado is nearby, plus a video of a tornado.

Tornadoes
http://www.weatherwizkids.com/tornado.htm
This website is packed with information about tornadoes, plus safety tips and activities.

Thunderstorms and Tornadoes
http://eo.ucar.edu/webweather/tornado.html
This site has lots of information, plus games, stories, and activities. You can even make your own tornado in a jar!

Glossary

damage: harm to buildings and other objects

masses: large amounts

rotate: to turn around a center point, like the way a wheel turns

supercells: very powerful thunderstorms

thunderstorm: a storm that has thunder and lightning

tornado: a dangerous, spinning windstorm

updraft: rising air

wind shear: a difference in speed or direction between two masses of air

Index